Principles of Leadership for Women

Gail Mays

Copyright © 2005 by Gail Mays

Published by Word for Life, Gardena, CA

All rights reserved. No part of this publication may be reproduced, stored in a retrieval system, or transmitted in any form or by any means without the prior permission of the publisher, except as provided by USA copyright law.

All Scripture quotations, unless otherwise indicated, are taken from the *King James Version Bible. Public Domain* . Copyright © 1982 by Thomas Nelson, Inc. Scripture quotations marked NIV are taken from the Holy Bible, New International Version . Used by permission. All rights reserved.

ISBN 0-9761478-2-3

Printed in the United States of America

Dedication

This book is dedicated first and foremost to the Lord Jesus—without a doubt He has had the greatest influence upon my life.

I would also like to dedicate this book to Kay Smith for patiently taking the time to teach me godly principles of leadership. It is through her example that I came to know and understand the unique call that God had placed upon my life to lead women. She has poured countless hours of her time and energy in to my life and into the lives of many other Pastors' wives. I am eternally grateful to her for teaching me to love and trust the Word of God for every situation in life.

Table of Contents

A Call to Ministry 7
What Is Required of Me? 9
Deal Thoroughly with Sin 11
Walking in Victory 13
Maintain a Strong Devotional Life 19
Keep the Right Perspective
on Trials and Pain 23
Never Own Anything 29
Never Defend Yourself 33
Never Verbally Pass On Anything
That Will Hurt Someone 35
Never Accept Any Glory 39
Love God's People 41
Pray, Pray, Pray 43
Conclusion 47
Notes 49

A Call to Ministry

It has been well over 25 years since I received my calling into the ministry. I was a young Christian at the time, but I can remember it as if it were today. I felt so overwhelmed and inadequate! Yet deep within my heart, I knew that the commitment I had made to Jesus Christ was genuine, and I wanted to do *whatever* was required of me. So, with all my heart I said "yes" to the call of God. Little did I know all that God had planned for me in the years ahead!

Serving God is an absolutely wonderful thing when we understand what it is and how God wants us to do it. He definitely has a plan for us to follow. I must admit, though, that when I first began in ministry I didn't have a clear picture of what was required of me. As a result, I became easily frustrated and often questioned my calling. Now, many years (or is it *tears?*) later, I have learned some principles that have helped me, and my desire is to share these with you.

As I sat under the instruction of both Chuck and Kay Smith, I gleaned principles over the years that I learned to apply as I served the Lord. None of them is unique; they are principles found in God's Word. But the way they were shared was practical and real. So many times this helped me understand better what was required of me in my calling. Often, what the Smiths shared with me was exactly what I needed to keep going and not quit.

If you're reading this booklet, then you, too, are looking for direction. You're wondering, just as I did, exactly what's required of you. I'd like to share with you some of the things that have helped me in my position in ministry. I pray that you will be instructed and encouraged as you read what I've written. Most of all, I pray that you will apply these principles. God's Word is clear, and He's simply looking for those who'll follow Him.

What Is Required of Me?

"Let a man so account of us, as of the ministers of Christ, and stewards of the mysteries of God. Moreover it is required in stewards, that a man be found faithful."
1 Corinthians 4:1-2

So often we feel a call of God upon our lives, yet we're left wondering, "What does this mean, and what will be required of me?" In 1 Corinthians, the apostle Paul reminds us that this call simply means that we are ministers of Christ. In other words, your position is one of a servant. God has raised you up to serve *Him*. Ministry is a privilege, and God has called you to serve "for such a time as this." The higher up in leadership, the more you serve. At times much will be required of you. The question each person must ask is, "Will I go all the way to Calvary?" Or will you only serve as far as you are comfortable? Remember what the Bible says about those who really want to be great—they must become a servant of all!

The Word declares that you are a minister called to share the mysteries of Christ. With that responsibility, a requirement is that you must be found faithful. Let's begin by looking at some principles that will direct you in being a faithful servant.

Oh may all who come behind us find us faithful.
May the fire of our devotion light their way.
May the footprints that we leave, lead them to believe.
And the lives we live inspire them to obey
Oh may all who come behind us find us faithful.
Donna Otto[1]

Deal Thoroughly with Sin

"Let not sin therefore reign in your mortal body, that ye should obey it in the lusts thereof."
Romans 6:12

The very first requirement of a faithful steward is that she must be willing to deal thoroughly with any sin in her life. It is required of you to live above reproach. In Romans we are exhorted to not let sin reign in our bodies. Christ must reign because He is the Preeminent One. For the woman whose desire is to be fit for the Master's use, this means that there must not be any bondage to sin. You should strive to become full-grown in the Lord, and sin that would stunt your growth must not mark your life. Ask God for a quickening concerning sin. Others may have more freedom to do particular things, but God requires of you a different life—a pure life. In purity there is power. A pure life becomes a powerful instrument in God's hands. A pure life doesn't taint God's work. Eternity can be poured through you because you've accepted the special call God has on your life. Although your natural abilities may be limited, you are supernaturally unlimited! When people view your life, they should not be able to see bad habits that have overcome you; instead, they must see that you have victory over sin.

A Father's cry goes out
Throughout the land today,
Who can find a virtuous woman,
In this world's moral decay?
In times when almost anything
Is acceptable to do,
A pure and godly influence
Is hard to find, it's true.
And yet the Father searches
The hearts of those He loves,
To find the ones whose hearts
Are fixed on things above.

Walking in Victory

"Now thanks be unto God, which always causeth us to triumph in Christ . . ."
2 Corinthians 2:14

VICTORY OVER DOUBT

"And straightway the father of the child cried out, and said with tears, Lord, I believe; help thou mine unbelief."
Mark 9:24

Walking in victory does not mean that you won't struggle with sin, doubt, or discouragement at times. It does mean that you will not give up on a situation, circumstance, or problem until you get the victory. It means being convinced that the work God has begun in you He will complete. It means having a conviction that because of past victories God has seen you through that He will sustain you during your present circumstance as well. You have the unshakable confidence that God is able to work all things for His good, using it to conform you into the image and likeness of Jesus. There's no doubt that you are limited, but you serve a God who is limitless—a God of the impossible! The opposite of a life of victory is a life of defeat, doubt, and discouragement. What good are you to others if you are not experiencing victory yourself? You must not be satisfied until you get victory over anything that is besetting you. When you know the way of escape, you can then lead others to experience this wonderful freedom in Christ.

Victory over Past

> *"Therefore if any man be in Christ, he is a new creature: old things are passed away; behold, all things are become new."*
> 2 Corinthians 5:17

To walk in victory also means that your past no longer has a hold on you. The greatest tool of the enemy is to constantly bring up your past. By doing this he somehow convinces you that you're not worthy to be a servant of the Lord. Beware of his tactics! Jesus Christ in you is what qualifies you to serve. Your past is covered in the blood, and it no longer stands in the way of what you can do for the Lord. Thanks be unto God who always causes you to triumph! As you stand in victory and refuse to let your past have a hold on you, others will be encouraged and will follow your example!

Victory over Thoughts

> *"Finally, brethren, whatsoever things are true, whatsoever things are honest, whatsoever things are just, whatsoever things are pure, whatsoever things are lovely, whatsoever things are of good report; if there be any virtue, and if there be any praise, think on these things."*
> Philippians 4:8

To walk in victory means that you bring your thought life under control. Thoughts are an amazing thing. If you can change a woman's way of thinking, you can change her whole outlook on life! Thoughts are the last frontier that must be conquered, and this takes a lifetime of work. As women, it seems that the smallest word can set us off or cause discouragement. Your thoughts will govern your life and will decide the condition of your heart. If you allow your thoughts to run away with you and to go unchecked, it won't be long before you'll be doing and saying things you said you'd never do! Remember that we've been given the power to close the door and turn from thoughts that are not pleasing to the Lord. Learn to recognize the fiery darts of the enemy that attack your mind. Don't go into Satan's arena—to go there is foolish. When tempted to entertain destructive, disturbing, or distracting thoughts, cast them on the Lord. Learn to turn your cares into prayers so you won't be hindered in your service. I've learned to tell myself immediately, "Don't go there, Gail!" This reminds me that I need to put a stop to my wrong thinking and instead think on things that are right, pure, and lovely.

A.W. Tozer said you *must* bring your thoughts under control; ". . . if not they will turn your mind into a wilderness where every foul beast will freely roam and weeds will overtake your garden."[2] Plant and sow good thoughts because bad thoughts can be very damaging. Thoughts affect your moods and set the course of your day and your attitude in serving others. Thoughts are powerful—no wonder you need to wash yourself in the blood of the Lamb! Saturate your mind in the Word. When you are living in the Word of God, there is no limit to your thoughts of peace, mercy, and goodness. Remember that you've been given the mind of Christ. To be fit for the Master's use, it's important for you to think as He thinks. You must put out thoughts that are your old nature. You must put out thoughts that are destructive and be very careful of worldly thinking. Instead, entertain thoughts that are good and godly. Put on what I call Philippians 4:8 thinking!

Before the winds that blow do cease, teach me to dwell within Thy calm: Before the pain has passed in peace, give me, my God, to sing a psalm. Let me not lose the chance to prove the fulness of enabling love. O Love of God, do this for me: maintain a constant victory.
Amy Carmichael [3]

Maintain a Strong Devotional Life

"But one thing is needful: and Mary hath chosen that good part, which shall not be taken away from her."
Luke 10:42

If there was one thing I could tell women today, it would be to develop and maintain a strong devotional life. I'm so thankful that in the early days of my ministry, Kay Smith laid the foundation for a successful ministry, teaching me the importance of daily spending time in the Word. She was absolutely right! I can still hear her saying, "If you don't do anything else, do this one thing!" So I made a commitment in my own heart that God's Word would be my number one passion, that every day I would spend quiet time with Jesus. It was my heart's desire then. It is the same today. Honestly, it has made all the difference!

My prayer is that you would do the same. It's not enough to just receive teaching from the pulpit—you must have a devotional life. It is the

Maintain a Strong Devotional Life

responsibility laid on your shoulders, not the law. Be wise and not weak. What will make you weak? Neglecting your devotional life! There's no way you will survive the attacks that will come in your position unless you have a strong devotional life. You don't need to be a spiritual giant; just be committed to the Word of God and spending time with Him. Make a vow to commit yourself to spend time *alone* with God *every* day. Ask yourself this question, "How can I be closer to Jesus today than I was yesterday?" As you do this, you will develop a love relationship with the Lord that you can't live without.

You must hear God speaking to you for yourself. The more you understand the Word, obey it, and apply it to your situation, the greater will be your spiritual growth. Be careful not to deny the study of the Word to "do things." This happened to Martha. She became busy doing so many things except the "main thing." Guard the "Mary" part of you. This is the first place the enemy will attack. Read the Word, pray, and wait until God speaks to you. Remember, it's not the amount of time that matters. What matters is that your time is undistracted. God wants to use ordinary women to do extraordinary work, but you must spend time with Him. If you'll be a Mary first, you'll be the best Martha anyone has ever seen. Guard your Mary's heart.

> *One thing is needful, oh my Father,*
> *One thing is needful, oh my God.*
> *That I sit at Your feet and pour out my love,*
> *This thing is needful, oh my Lord,*
> *This thing is needful, oh my Lord.*[4]

Keep the Right Perspective on Trials and Pain

"For I reckon that the sufferings of this present time are not worthy to be compared with the glory which shall be revealed in us."
Romans 8:18

Because your ministry is one of mentoring, you can't possibly teach others until you gain the right perspective on trials! I can't promise you a life or a ministry without pain. To tell you the truth, you may even have more trials than others do—even trials that you do not necessarily deserve. But what I can promise is that God never wastes your pain. He will use every trial to make you more prepared and fit for the Master's use. Oh, if I could only convince you that your difficult circumstances are not a mistake; rather, they're allowed in your life for a divine purpose. I can remember hearing Kay Smith say, "I can faithfully tell you there is not a test or trial that I have ever gone through, no matter how insignificant, that if

I turned it over to the Lord He didn't do something eternally profitable with it. I have learned more about the Lord God through tests and trials than any other way." As a leader, you must see God's hand in all that comes your way! God is working something in you that only this trial can accomplish. What you go through is for the benefit of the body of Christ. Trials change you. It is through them that you grow and mature in your walk. In time, the trial will pass, but what you were while in the trial will remain. As a leader, it is so important that you willingly and joyfully accept your circumstances and allow God to complete His purpose.

There are two kinds of lives—the plowed life and the fallow life. "Miracles follow the plowed life." You must be willing to allow the Lord to plow your life and take out anything that is not pleasing to Him. As a leader fit for the Master's use, you are called to cooperate with Him. A faithful steward gives God the freedom to take out anything He wants from your life—even good things. As you comply with Him and allow Him to freely work, He can accomplish the work *He* wants to do in and through you.

Principles of Leadership for Women

Keep the Right Perspective

A fallow life results when a woman does not have the right perspective on pain and trials. A fallow (unplowed) life takes much work and results in very little. I can't count how many times over the years I have wanted to remove myself from the ministry because of the personal and private pain I was going through. But the Lord had me remain right where I was and continue to serve Him faithfully. I urge you, don't waste your pain! Don't wait for your pain to pass before you do anything for God; instead, let God use you right where you are.

Don't ever be afraid of a life that's broken. The more your personal life is broken, the more your life will declare, "Glory to God." If He's plowing, it's because He wants to do a deeper work. Rocks will arise even in a plowed field, so God will continually work to bring these to the surface and rid your life of them. The work of the Lord is to strip us of self-confidence, not self-worth. Welcome the trial and embrace it as from the very hand of God. If you want miracles to follow your plowed life, then you must be willing to be stripped. The times of testing show you just how much you have an inclination to trust in your own abilities. Your own self-confidence can equal the death of your ministry. Therefore, the Lord, in His love, tests you so that self doesn't reign. He strips away what you once had confidence in. Plowing allows Him to take away all that you are dependent upon other than Him.

A faithful servant is willing to be plowed because being plowed will help you produce much fruit. One of the fruits developed through trials is compassion. It wasn't that long ago that the Lord taught me a precious lesson in this specific area. My relationship with my daughter was quite strained, and I was feeling awkward around her. The more I wanted to grow close, the more distant we seemed to become. I even felt that she was pushing me away. Although I knew better, I began to feel sorry for myself and develop a "woe is me" syndrome (or is that sin-drome!). It wasn't long before I was crying out to the Lord to do something. As soon as I had quieted my heart, He was faithful to speak to me. "Gail, could you just forget about yourself for a minute and consider what she's been through?" So I did. In my mind I vividly recalled November 1, 1996. It was a day that has forever changed my daughter's life.

Keep the Right Perspective 27

Gang violence had struck the streets of Los Angeles once again—something that had become almost a common occurrence. Some unfortunate kid had lost his life. His body was found in the usual gang execution place in the local foothills. A motorist driving by early in the morning discovered him in a pool of his own blood. This unfortunate 23-year-old young man had been shot 14 times! Police said that there was no sign of struggle. Yes, gang violence had struck again. Except this time, this "unfortunate stranger" was somebody to me. He was my son-in-law. My precious Heather had lost her husband. My grandson would never see his daddy again.

As the Lord pierced my heart, I knew immediately that I had to keep reaching out to her, to be caring but not controlling, allowing God's Spirit time and space to heal her broken heart. I thanked the Lord for reminding me to consider her and not myself. Shortly thereafter, my daughter and I went and had a cup of coffee, and all of a sudden I saw her in a completely different light. Something came over me and my heart was flooded with compassion for her. By God's grace, I was able to look beyond myself and my hurt and see her heavy load. Since that day, my relationship with her has changed—and not only with her, but also with others. My trial produced in me a heart of compassion. Suddenly I was able to put myself in other people's shoes and was moved to reach out and help them however I could.

God has allowed your painful circumstance. Praise the Lord He's plowing! That means He wants to use you to touch the lives of His people. God can't use someone who isn't broken. His people are too precious and too frail. When you are plowed, you will become more gracious, tender, and compassionate. You'll become more like Jesus! He's making your life have rich soil so you'll not only take in but also give out to others. That's your call to ministry—to help others. A field that is worked over and plowed is ready for one thing—a bountiful harvest!

Never Own Anything

"But none of these things move me, neither count I my life dear unto myself, so that I might finish my course with joy, and the ministry, which I have received of the Lord Jesus, to testify the gospel of the grace of God."
Acts 20:24

As women we just love to possess things! But in God's Kingdom, you don't own anything! Everything you have belongs to Him, including your ministry. You don't own a position; you fill it! As a leader fit for the Master's use, you must rid yourself of the sense of possessing and controlling. If this tendency isn't kept in check, it will easily get out of control. We're to do what we do well, but we don't own any position or person. Remember that the very thing you hold onto you will lose. It's God's ministry, and He's simply given you charge. You're a steward or a caretaker of what God owns. You're to be a faithful steward with what He's given, but never lose sight that He owns it all.

Principles of Leadership for Women

The leader must keep in mind that it's God's work, done God's way, for God's glory, and in God's time. God has raised you into the position you have, and you are not to pound in any stakes, claiming a position or territory as "mine." To do this will cause you to neglect raising up others or to quit mentoring because only *you* can do this thing. Your intent may be right, but you cannot own anything. Remember that you're a steward. Ministry is yours to fulfill, not possess.

God moves people where He wants them. Positions change, and people come and go. A faithful steward puts in her mind that everything belongs to God and she does not claim ownership over anything. Keeping this mind-set is crucial for those entrusted with Kingdom work. It's crucial that we hold things loosely and give God time and space to work. Allow Him the freedom to move people, places, and things to accomplish His will. Never get too comfortable in what you're doing. God doesn't want you so comfortable you no longer have to trust Him. He will keep you in a place in which you are constantly challenged to walk by faith trusting in Him. If you can't walk by faith, how will you teach others to do this?

Keep in mind that when things change, many times the enemy begins to attack. He whispers his accusations: "You didn't do that well enough, so it was taken away and given to someone better." He knows all too well that our fleshly nature says that change equals a personal indictment against us. This is not true! If it isn't what we think is a good change or it's a change that will be hard for us, we tend to take it personally and negatively. Be careful of this. Remember your vulnerability and remain flexible, teachable, and moveable! God owns ministry and you don't, so separate your feelings from what God desires. If He's changing or shifting you, it's because He wants to do a new work or He's putting you in a place of service to increase your gifts. You are simply His laborer, His instrument, His steward called to tend His flock in whatever place or capacity He desires. Your identity is in Christ, not in your position. Your position doesn't make you who you are; it's Christ in you that's important.

In the midst of change, keep yourself and your motives pure. Continue to deal thoroughly with any sin that arises. To allow sin to go unchecked will be your downfall. Sin puts you down and out of ministry! Enjoy what God gives you to do. Pass on your gifts and abilities to others so they too can enjoy being a part of God's work. Remember that you are a steward and God owns it all. Resist the temptation to hold on to anything. After all, why do you want to own this tiny piece of property when God wants to give you so much more?

No wound? No scar?
Yet, as the Master shall the servant be,
And pierced are the feet that follow Me;
But thine are whole: can he have followed far
Who has no wound nor scar?
Amy Carmichael [5]

Never Defend Yourself

*"He was oppressed, and He was afflicted,
yet He opened not His mouth."*
Isaiah 53:7

Another checkpoint for the steward of God is this: Never defend yourself. In striving for excellence in ministry, there will be risks taken and mistakes made. It's then that people will criticize you the most. To be defensive is a natural tendency when others criticize or evaluate your work. You'll instinctively want to tell your side of the story so the "truth" can be known by all. You will never keep yourself 100 percent clear of criticism so determine now that it's the Lord you must please!

Don't allow yourself to become angry in confrontations. It isn't about you; it's about tending the flock. God is your defense. If your heart is right, your actions and decisions that follow will be right. Keep in mind that there is always room for improvement. Walk humbly before your God.

Don't forget you're in a spiritual battle and the enemy is seeking to entrap you! Expect his attacks and know the true source of your problems. You are on the front lines, possibly even in enemy territory, and you cannot please everybody. Satan knows your weaknesses so don't be drawn in by his tactics. Stand firm and secure in Christ and refuse the temptation to be defensive! Remember that, by the subtle stabs of others, the enemy will try to knock you down, but he cannot knock you out! Nothing can touch you that will prosper because God is in control. Let Him direct you! Ask yourself, "What would Jesus do?" Would He be angry or personally offended? Would the One whom the Bible calls a "worm" and a "lamb" try to verbally prove His point and defend Himself? God is your defense! Keep yourself thoroughly cleansed from sin. Never defend yourself. That's what being a faithful steward is all about.

> *I will be with you, in joy and in pain.*
> *Your cry for mercy echoes My name.*
> *Now and forever I'll be at hand.*
> *I will be with you, I will be with you,*
> *for that's who I am.* [6]

Never Verbally Pass On Anything That Will Hurt Someone

"She openeth her mouth with wisdom; and in her tongue is the law of kindness."
Proverbs 31:26

Another requirement of a faithful steward is that she must choose her words carefully. Because you are in a position of authority, the words you use carry authority. Words said to the wrong person or in the wrong spirit can wound deeply. Think before you speak. Just because you have information does not mean you have the freedom to share it. And if you do share, you don't necessarily have to share *all* you know. Ask God what you should share and how you should share. He will give you discernment. All too often we say far too much. It's better to wait and be sure than to speak hastily and do damage to another person. You are a steward. You must be careful with God's people. A leader fit for the Master's use will be required to guard her tongue.

Confidentiality is of utmost importance! Many times as a leader, you will be given information that others do not have. Can you be trusted with that information? Does someone else have to be careful of what she tells you for fear that you will repeat it to others? Be someone who can be trusted with words. Only share what you have the freedom to share and remember that it must never be used to hurt another. Before you speak, try what Amy Carmichael suggests, asking yourself these three questions: "Is it true? Is it kind? Is it necessary?"

Many times you will be the one who directly communicates with the people. When you give orders to others, be careful. Don't demand things of people. Instead, ask them. This will ensure that you are communicating in the right spirit. It's your responsibility to take plans and what's discussed to the women in the same heart as it was given to you. Paul sent certain ones to share because he trusted they would share his heart in the matter. Know the leader's heart in a matter and make sure that is what's communicated above all else. Build a bridge between the people and your leader.

A Couple of Warnings for Stewards

First, be careful in your jesting. Do not get careless and laugh and tease at the expense of another. People are frail and can easily be hurt, especially by those whom they respect most. Be careful especially what you say when another is not present. A good rule of thumb to help you avoid succumbing to talking about another is to remember that if you can't say something nice, don't say it at all.

Second, there are no secrets when it comes to sin, wrong attitudes, or wrongdoing! It's your responsibility to bring information to those over you. If sin is involved, if there are shadows of misconduct, or if you suspect wrongdoing, you are *not* to "protect" others. To keep to yourself information about another's misconduct is to hold an incredible burden that you are not meant to carry. Leaders are to live above reproach, and their lives are an open book for all to see. Because leaders carry the responsibility to direct others in the way of the Lord, their life must be right with God.

Principles of Leadership for Women

Never Verbally Pass On Anything

If I belittle those whom I'm called to serve, talk of their weak points in contrast perhaps with what I think of as my strong points; if I adopt a superior attitude, forgetting "Who made thee to differ?" and "What hast thou that thou hast not received?" then I know nothing of Calvary Love.
Amy Carmichael [7]

Never Accept Any Glory

*"I am the Lord: that is My name:
and My glory will I not give to another . . ."*
Isaiah 42:8

Glory belongs to God, and your position is to bring Him attention. It's God's work, done God's way, for God's glory! As a leader fit for the Master's use, beware of pride! It can be a horrible monster or a purring kitten, but nevertheless beware! It's never far away and always ready to attack. You will battle pride every day. Self loves to be praised. Never allow yourself to think that you're irreplaceable. Remember that it's not how great you are; it's how great *He* is in you! You're simply a clay pot chosen by the Master to be used. It's not the container people should notice but rather what's inside the container! When you serve the Lord, what shines most? You or Christ in you?

Although you must be careful about pride, you also must learn to receive praise graciously. Often people just need to express what they feel so that it becomes reality. Nothing is insignificant when it changes a life. So graciously receive praise but don't let it go to your head. It's good counsel to take those things said to you, thank God for the token that confirms you are right where God wants you, and then forget about it. Don't share what was said with another; forget it and go on with His work for His glory. I love what Corrie ten Boom says about receiving the praises of people. She says to receive what they say as one would a bouquet of flowers and then simply to throw it at the feet of Jesus as your precious offering to Him.

Warning! When you try to please people more than the Lord, He will expose your frailty. Serve to please the Lord above all else. It's impossible to please all people. Eventually it will become a trap and hinder you from doing what the Lord wants you to do. Impress God and not people; then you can be sure He will get the glory due His holy name!

> *Glory to Jesus wonderful Savior!*
> *Glory to Jesus, the One I adore.*
> *Glory to Jesus wonderful Savior!*
> *Glory to Jesus, and praise evermore.*
> Hymn

Love God's People

"Love never fails . . ."
1 Corinthians 13:8 (NIV)

For the leader fit for the Master's use, loving His people is not an option! With your call to service comes the incredible challenge to love the people of God. The greatest need in the world today is genuine love. Many people grow up in such fractured homes that they never know what true love is. We have the awesome opportunity to show them the love of God. Faithful stewards learn to encircle people. Don't make rules and regulations that shut people out; instead, widen your circle and allow them in.

God's agape love is big enough to include everyone. This means accepting others just as they are. No matter what their faults or shortcomings, love them. Don't put a burden on people just because you have a need. Instead, pray and ask God to send you the right people for what you need. There's a place for all His children to serve!

Be careful what you share about another who is not meeting your expectations. Don't taint their character by what you say. Don't allow yourself to get an attitude toward God's people. Instead of getting frustrated at them, pray and ask the Lord to help you discover their gifts and then put them where they will shine.

> *Lord, give me eyes*
> *That I may see*
> *Lest I, as people will,*
> *Should pass someone's Calvary*
> *And think it just a hill.*
> Unknown

Pray, Pray, Pray

"Be careful for nothing; but in every thing by prayer and supplication with thanksgiving let your requests be made known unto God."
Philippians 4:6

The choice is prayer or paralysis. If this doesn't seem like much of a choice, it isn't! If you want to be effective in your ministry, you must pray. I personally feel the greatest ministry that women have today is prayer! In the Word, we're told to worry about nothing—not *one thing*—and to commit everything to God in prayer. Instead, too often, we worry about everything and pray about nothing! Soon you'll realize that you're spiritually paralyzed. Prayer is not pointless nor is it powerless. In fact, prayer is so powerful it can set captives free and can demolish strongholds—but first, it has to be utilized.

When I take my grandson for a ride in the car, the first thing I always tell him is to put on his seatbelt. He says to me in return, "Grandma, you buckle up for safety too!" Once we both have our seatbelts on, we head off in the car. I wouldn't begin to think about going anywhere with my "precious cargo" unless I had first made sure he was safe. Putting on seatbelts is automatic for us. Prayer should be the same way! It's your safety weapon. It's a must that you make it a priority before you head into the day and your work for the Lord. You may not know what you'll encounter on the road of life, but you can know for sure that prayer will keep you safe!

Have you forgotten what prayer can accomplish? I'm so thankful that early on in ministry the example was set for me to make prayer my first response. By doing so, I immediately get God involved in the situation! Because of prayer, I never have to say, "There's nothing I can do." Prayer is powerful, and it accomplishes much for those entrusted with God's people and God's holy work. If you don't do anything else, pray. Make a resolution right now to commit everything to the Lord in prayer. Not just the big things, the major problems or worries in your life, but *everything*. Spend some time with the Lord, telling Him all your cares and concerns. Exchange those heartaches, those things that paralyze you, for His incredible peace and wait upon Him until you know His heart and mind in a matter. Pray that He would teach you how to instantly bring things before His throne.

> *Thou art coming to a King,*
> *Large petitions with thee bring:*
> *For His grace and power are such,*
> *None can ever ask too much!*
> Hymn

Conclusion

"And let us not be weary in well doing: for in due season we shall reap, if we faint not."
Galatians 6:9

Leadership is a high calling and a privilege. With that privilege comes responsibility. But if you follow the instructions in God's Word, you will avoid many of the pitfalls that the enemy lays out to entrap you. Remember that his greatest tool is to try and make those called into ministry discouraged and ineffective so they can't accomplish a great work for God. Some of the saddest experiences I've had in ministry are when people fall out of the race. Don't give in to the enemy's tactics. Peter says it best when he reminds us, just before his own death, to give diligence to make your calling and election sure so you will never fall (2 Peter 1:10). So, beloved ones, stand firm in your calling!

What an awesome privilege we've been given as stewards of the mysteries of God! There is no greater service here on earth than to spend your

Conclusion

life for what matters most. Every day you serve, someone's eternity is at stake. Give out the Word. Let Jesus in you increase and you decrease. One day not too far away you will receive the greatest honor that can ever be given to any steward. You will stand in the presence of Almighty God and hear Him say, "Well done, my good and faithful servant. Enter into the joy of the Lord." Now that's a reason to serve!

> *"Be thou an example of the believers, in word, in conversation, in charity, in spirit, in faith, in purity."*
> 1 Timothy 4:12

Notes

1. Donna Otto, *Between Women of God* (Eugene, OR: Harvest House, 1995), p. 180.

2. A.W. Tozer, *Gems from Tozer* (Bromley, Kent, England: Send the Light Trust, 1969).

3. Amy Carmichael, *Rose from Brier* (Fort Washington, PA: Christian Literature Crusade, 1971).

4. Kirk Dearman, Maranatha! Music, 1983

5. Amy Carmichael, *Toward Jerusalem* (Fort Washington, PA: Christian Literature Crusade, 1977), p. 85.

6. "I Will Be with You" (Bill Batstone).

7. Amy Carmichael, *If* (London: Dohnavur Fellowship, 1938), p. 14.

*Other Resources Available
by Gail Mays*

HOMEWORK STUDIES
1. John
2. Acts
3. Seven Churches of Asia Minor
4. Women of the Bible (Part 1)
5. Women of the Bible (Part 2)

Tapes/CDs also available

OTHER BOOKLETS
Planning Events for Your Women's Ministry

Jewelry Box of Joy *(a 31-day devotional through the book of Philippians)*

HOW TO ORDER
Contact Calvary Chapel South Bay Women's Ministry at (310) 352-3333, ext. 245.